From the library of:

The Mirrored Clubs of Hell

Arcade Publishing / New York

LITTLE, BROWN AND COMPANY

The MIRRORED CLUBS *of* HELL

POEMS *by* GERRIT HENRY

With an Introduction by JOHN ASHBERY

First edition

Some of these poems have appeared in *Poetry, The Paris Review,
The American Poetry Review, The Yale Lit, Columbia: A Magazine of Poetry
and Prose, Brooklyn Review, Mudfish, Oink!, Mothers of Mud,
Broadway II,* and *The Bad Henry Review.*

Library of Congress Cataloging-in-Publication Data

Henry, Gerrit.
  The mirrored clubs of hell / by Gerrit Henry; with an
introduction by John Ashbery.—1st ed.
    p. cm.
  ISBN 1-55970-099-8 (hc)
  ISBN 1-55970-100-5 (pbk)
  I. Title.
  PS3558.E49735M57 1991
  811'.54—dc20   90-49067

Published in the United States
by Arcade Publishing, Inc., New York,
a Little, Brown company

HC: 10 9 8 7 6 5 4 3 2 1
PB: 10 9 8 7 6 5 4 3 2 1

BP

*Published simultaneously in Canada
by Little, Brown & Company (Canada) Limited*

Printed in the United States of America
Designed by Marc Cheshire

For James and Jane Henry

Contents

Intermission

Recently

Acknowledgments

The author wishes to acknowledge the aid and support of Ellen Adler, Richard and Jeannette Seaver, John Ashbery, Marc Cohen, Susan Baran, Janice Henry, Eugene Richie, Rosanne Wasserman, John Wells, David Lehman, Darragh Park, Jill Hoffman, Richard Roth, Darryl Hine, Patricia Storace, John Ash, James Schuyler, and Professor Kenneth Koch.

Introduction

GERRIT HENRY's poems are by turns, sometimes even simultaneously, bitter and very funny, wry and ecstatic, harrowing and soothing. His subjects are pain and alienation, TV and the movies, relationships with friends, lovers, and parents; life in New York City and the price its transitory pleasures exact; cruising in Village bars and celebrating one's birthday in a psychiatric ward; God and death and AIDS. At times it seems that he is about to tell us more about himself than he should ("I've gotten fat to discourage AIDS"), but he has the knack of stopping just before he does so. (His stops are incredible and heart-wrenching.) But in fact he isn't telling us about himself to make us feel bad, or good, as some confessional poets have done; he's not telling us about himself, not even telling. Witnessing might be a better word, except that it sounds pretentious and constrained. Instead his rhymes and rhythms are those of the ballads of two poets he particularly admires: Cole Porter and Lorenz Hart, yet always slightly off balance. The metrical shoe never falls precisely at the place where we had anticipated it would. This is but one of many strategies toward an openness amounting to suspense, an unresolved chord at the end. And the subjects listed above aren't precisely subjects, but loci that stake out the territory he travels through, a Dante adrift without a Virgil in the mirrored clubs of hell and their surrounding cityscape: a world he never made but has acclimated himself to for the time being. No, the subject of his poetry is poetry itself, in the broadest sense of the word: a voice that moves toward and away from us and finally just stops, leaving us with the feeling that we have just sensed life, though we would be hard put to analyze it—and why not? Life is like that.

Perhaps the quintessential Henry poem is "The Watchers," in

which the poet is writing the poem and at the same time watching on TV a horror movie so bad that even he considers abandoning it ("I am / shocked and outraged / By the sheer ugliness / Of it all..."). But..."Will I turn it / Off? Probably, no. / I am lonely. And, in some / Subtle, subterranean way, / The movie gives me courage, / Just by its viciousness." But he doesn't stop there: at the end he is turning back to the typewriter to "write you, and me, /An alternative, / Write away the horror, / Write away the blood, / The inevitable, quick progression / Of another American night." In talking about writing an "alternative," Henry actually does so. The horror—and humor—of being trapped with a horror movie that can't even manage to be horrifying is quietly subsumed into "another American night" as the voice stops and the film continues to glimmer for a few seconds, like the point of light at the center of a television screen after you turn it off. Celluloid blood and gore, the poet's unrequited love affair with pop culture and his brief apostrophe to an unnamed "you," the traditional trappings of poetry and narrative which Henry is happy to avail himself of when they can further the work—all dissolve in a closure like that of a Brucknerian or Mahlerian adagio, a moment as transparent as a bubble that is about to burst. This is the splendor of his poetry, which is of a kind we haven't seen before.

JOHN ASHBERY

Early '70s

Night Skies

The evening star is rising.
Nearby stands surprising
Orion with his club,
A handsome Beelzebub.

Alert to the song of Venus—
"Nothing can come between us"—
Is Justice with her scales.
Through heavenly hills and dales

Runs the twinkling Milky Way.
Out of the light of day,
The moon is a bit of cotton
Never to be forgotten.

Just as pictorial
Is Jupiter's bright aureole.
As Haley's Comet streaks by,
Tiny Pluto sneaks by.

The Big and Little Dippers
Look like rhinestone slippers,
And bright orbs everywhere
Trace the path of the Great Bear.

Now the evening star is fading.
Mars is through parading.
As the Archer shoots his arrow
To the morning song of a sparrow

A pink glow lights the sky.
Soon the sun will hang high
From Nebraska to Carolina,
And the Twins will smile on China.

Questions and Answers

1
Could I stop loving you?
Is a city editor smarter than his reporters?

Will I see you tonight?
How much power can you assume without losing control?

Do I love you?
Was I happy as a child?

Could I live without you?
Is philosophy a science?

Could I live without you?
Does spring have a name?

2
Could I do without you?
Can the wind part the hair?

Do I miss you?
Are there oases in the Sahara?

Should I kiss you?
Does the sky get plenty of light?

Do I want you?
Can the sun burn the skin?

3

Am I serious about you?
Have you ever seen a sparrow walk?

Do you love me?
How often are the times of day?

Are you mine?
How many people went to work today?

Do you love me?
Or is life just a balloon trip?

Night and Day

They tell me you're beautiful: I'm game.
But it's seeing you later I'm nostalgic for this morning.
Both our eyes uplifted, seeing straight.
To have left a moment ago is to have made a date.

Because you've got the power. I have a conviction.
We throw fate to the winds without a sideways glance.
All at once I'm doing something original:
Giving luck a break while I still have the chance.

"Look before you fall" was the truth of the matter.
We did, and the butterfly of passion was freed.
Now no more concerning yourself with how to relax:
This time the possibilities only gloss the facts.

Pretty up the picture by telling the truth,
But there's nothing remarkable in living out our glory.
How do we do it? That's not for us to say,
And with our not refusing to, we solve the story.

Do I remember? That's an unusual question.
Your being here as proof is a clue to answer:
"We were out on the floor. The orchestra was playing.
I put my arms around you and we held the dancer."

My life before that was little more than enjoyable.
At the crack of dawn, birds would sing and scold me.
The jig was up: you held the winning number.
I drew aside the curtains. The world was too big to hold me.

The way you fall asleep
As if nothing were ending
As if nothing were pending
Just like a child

Like a promise you keep
With all of your powers
Not counting the hours
Subdued and wild

About the way you sleep
As causal as wishing
Terrified, gone fishing
With me beside you

Thinking it comes too cheap
Watching the nightlight
Your eyes shut tight
With nothing to hide you

But the way you fell asleep
Like the wind busy seeding
Or a bird hectically feeding
Too absorbed to care

Without so much as a peep
It's a disease for sure
And you've found the cure
Just lying there

You jerk a bit in your sleep
But it doesn't matter
There are no hopes to shatter
For right now

Just many gains to reap
Projects to be forsaken
Nothing can be mistaken
You know how

The way you stay asleep
Sweaty, basking
Impenetrable, unasking
Just like that

Just having made the leap
Somewhere beyond enjoyment
All fatigue at your deployment
The canary and the cat

The way you fall asleep
Without even trying
Without even dying
Like a new religion

Making a clean sweep
Although you may not know it
You feel it and you show it
By your decision

To fall asleep
As though you were a poppy

The original, not the copy
Doting, disarmed

No ocean is as deep
Keeping a lifelong date
Knowing it's never too late
To sleep, unharmed

A Little Before Noon

Here's *National Geographic*
with a furry black and white
panda on the cover, just like
the one I had as a baby. Well,
not just like it—there's
a dull twinkle in this one's eyes

not unlike the one you get
when I ask, "What's wrong,
baby?" and you answer, "Nothing
is wrong," going to emotional bed

Another thing I had as a boy
and do again today is
grape gum, and was. It sits
across from the *National Geographic*
on the desk, its contents
partially ransacked, as I chew,
staring into space as if it were
a flashback. I remember standing by

the window at Clyde Road, chewing
grape gum, my mother off singing
somewhere, my panda propped bug-eyed
on the bed in my room. But it's
different now—today's flavor is
an acidic sour grape, while then it was
sweet, sweet as the moment after
I've talked you out of your mood and
we are both talking, making plans, major
ones, gum that was good enough to eat

The sonata playing has an amazing clarity.
Its beauty is just
and in its passion is a true hilarity.

The lyricism is in the lust.
The piano keeps up with the strings at a distance,
and they keep up, a careful trust,

followed by a passage of warm insistence.
Who knows when it will end?
The music's delicacy is in its persistence,

and the way the notes seem to tend
during the quiet gallop,
rounding the corner to a further bend.

Things aren't as bright as they seem,
they're better.
The other is a secondary theme.

The scherzo follows its course to the letter.
The abiding humor is heightened
until it's felt largely as a fetter.

The wit of the movement is thus lightened
by its harmonic piquancy.
The piano seems nicely frightened.

Silence maintains by its infrequency.
The viola player can relax
as the contrapuntal screw is tightened.

The last movement is a switch,
the cure that proves the curse,
culminating in a kind of leisurely twitch,

beyond perfect pitch.
Then it ends, the way a broken heart eventually mends,
for better or for worse.

A Thought for Today

1
Is that what you call making the bed? "Now look!"
Since morning the room has been messy with sunlight.
The mattress rests under an immovable ocean of quilt,
Strewn with pillows and a chance pajama top,

And it's all so dreamy, this thankless task.
"Why not just go in there and do it right?"
But I have to feel my way through this balmy Sunday.
At best, I can only grasp the bannister of afternoon,
Picking and choosing my steps as I crazily descend.
"When I get there what'll I do?"
Well, the leaves on the rubber plant are so many foreign flags.
The little linden tree has these aspirations.

2
Slowing down, the rocking horse reclaims it precarious poise,
As a little sunshine goes under the hooves.
Billy NoFun climbs off and storms away.
Down at the bottom of the sea, so much has been declared,

To be thrust upon us today, dripping with seaweed and salt,
Advancing until all you can see are enormous, bony legs
Awash in a down of light black hair.
Then the nickel drops. The telescope goes black.

3
"Sunday—is that what you call it?"
The breeze has its little joke, and blows.

"Have you seen my passport?
I need it for personal identification." Look everywhere
You think you might have misplaced it.
"I bet I find it somewhere special."
The light in the lilacs against the window is a love nest.
"Courage, pilgrims. Rhythms of reeds,

Of last chances straggling underwater make you reel,
But your passion is no, not altogether spent.
Faces appearing at the window mildly approve.
The twilight is hard. It is Lent."

Maybe so. But our dreams disorient us more
As over the years they jell into screams.
Right now, I feel a little sick from thinking.
The nutshell I put things in can get out of hand.

"What now, mariner? And what of it?"
The room is visibly increasing with age,
The stage of an increasingly peaceful set-to.
It no longer looks as if Blake had slept there,

But Keats. Tired of all that fame,
The sun sets, igniting a moment of intense change.
If there's something you always meant to do, but haven't,
Considering the hour, why not now?
Because you need sunlight and a passport for this, too?
Everything burgeons around you, sounds and sights
That leave you awestruck with their complete lack of cohesion
Or even incident. "You've never seen this photo of my house.

This is the back, and that's my old bedroom window,
To which that tree branch used to reach.
One night I just climbed out, shinnied down, and ran away."
Somehow, I'll make it all up to you.

Beloved Ingrate

Night, or what's left of it, is waning.
Less laughter is heard, less audible straining
At disquietude's leash. Yet the sense of something unfinished—
A ways to go—has not by any appraisal diminished.

You may regret it wholeheartedly in the morning
But that possibility is not a strong enough warning
To keep you from making your upcoming rounds
Through a region of indiscernible lights and sounds.

A moment's struggle, then the end of strife,
A lifetime in a moment of eternal life,
Are the experiences for which you are about to sue,
Alone, with all the others like you.

Recipient of a thousand conflicting reports,
You are about to trace the confusion to its source.
That there is going to be no other way
Is a fact attested to by the nearing break of day,

The far-off rumble of trucks, violet alleyways, cats,
Slinking along window ledges like rats.
Soon day will make its hard-won stand,
Claiming every bit of atmosphere and dry land

For itself. You persist in a different eventuality.
As sunlight is persuasive, so is darkness a reality
Exerting an equal, equally valid fascination
Over you who would, however irregularly, keep its station.

Unimaginable as it is, then, you will continue
In search of the one thing to both defeat and finally win you
What you most need, have had, and often will,
Every reserve of determination, luck and skill

Applied to meeting what lies ineluctably ahead.
Later, there will be your daily bread.
In the meantime, the waxing moon
Has its day. You will forget the great price soon.

Notorious

1
The big paranoia was no longer limited
to girl reporter alone at last with killer.
Things had gotten completely out of hand,

or it was just the law of equal distribution.
Everyone was infected, goon-faced,
lips buttoned like shifting acres of sand.

Throughout this purge in reverse, though,
I managed to keep the image
of your sacred, laughing face before me.

Let government bloat up like hydrogen, I thought.
You're where you are.
Let the think-men pointedly ignore me.

Reading between the lines of this new contract
as never before or since
I felt my own overwhelming uncertainty

about the terms to be a strange reward
on all but this one, unwritten point.
In time, everything else would stop hurting me,

but what I could depend on I knew I could least
afford to take for granted.
I could only tumble wide-eyed into bed with it.

The next morning there would be something
wrong with the water. The air hurt.
But we went ahead with it.

When my more suspicious friends offered a dissenting
opinion, I had a little trouble hearing them.
They had no audible voice

in this ancient, enormous chamber
where no match had ever been struck
and questions were only noise.

2
Sooner or later, though, we had
to surface for the dangling lure of supplies.
That sunny May morning we slept late

in the face of an infinitely slow
but universal chain reaction, one of the links
of which just happened to be this place, on this date.

All sleep and light, you left unawares for the
holidays. The hot afternoon passed by on stilts.
That evening I observed the strike,

but mechanically, no longer putting any
faith in its efficacy. A nice idea, it just
wasn't what things had ever been like.

The doubts arose again a little later,
the way you could sometimes still see Venus.
I walked up the broad, sweltering avenue

picking my way through the dogs
and the kids. With every uneasy step I took
I wanted to turn back to you,

catch you up in my arms, then just casually die.
Finally, though, by the simple law of propulsion
I found myself in the arcade of the new ministry,

my brain working overtime, like a pinwheel.
I had all I could do to keep from telling them,
but it stuck. When it was over, they were finished with me.

3
In the long run, the paranoia we all felt
had become the very weather.
Maybe that's why the sky was always green,

day and night, as if a vote had been taken
by word of mouth. It had all come out in the open.
Now, at long last, we could take in the unseen.

Back at base, the curtains blew in
a second at the window,
the only breeze I was to know all summer.

It made me think of what you said,
the ultimate admission of joy, which only made
present conditions seem that much glummer,

the thought of life without you,
the worst having come to pass,
and one of us inexplicably dead.

But when they burst into the room
you weren't among them, in person or in spirit.
And I knew briefly, I hadn't been misled.

The Lecturer's Aria

1
Always the first one to admit to
His difficulties along that line,
Tchaikovsky may never have written
A successful opera. The challenge, though,

Was such that he continued to return
To the form, making tonal adjustments
Here, trying to get rid of that
Confounded, trademark symphonic

Sound there. No dice, I think.
"Eugene Onegin" has its
Moments, especially the soaring
"Letter Song," but it remains

An obtuse, overripe work, a kind of
Grand operetta, complete with its famous
Waltz. "Queen of Spades" is
Strictly gorgeous. Now we have

"Maid of Orleans," the composer's
Love-letter to the life of the French
Saint and martyr. Not exactly medieval
In flavor, "Maid" misses the point

Of Joan's particular experience in time
Completely. Adapted by Tchaikovsky from
Schiller's apparently nonsensical verse drama,
And sung in unlikely Russian accents! Not

To mention Joan's flagrantly ahistorical
Fling with a Burgundian knight named
Lionel. All in all, "Maid of Orleans"
Seems not just a little jerky.

2
A florid love duet on the battlefield?
Joan of Arc as the Sleeping Beauty?
But, from the vocal evidence, it is
Beautiful—in parts, plentifully.

Listen—Joan and the people of
Orleans are caroling grandly
With one another. "Fires are seen in
The distance," read the liner notes.

"Thiebaut accuses Joan of
Consorting with evil spirits."
Sounds like Tchaikovsky could be
Accused of consorting with good

Ones. But is that in itself enough?
What about the rapaciousness and plague
That were everywhere in Joan's day?
There's more to come certainly—

Maybe Tchaikovsky will buckle down
As he gets further along—but then,
Why should he? What's wrong with
Able grandiosity and velvet melody,

This majestic and overarching beauty?
What if the French of the Middle
Ages had known how to waltz? The better
For us. Untrue to that

Kind of manic jaundice that was probably
The temper of the times, "The Maid"
Is overwhelmingly true to the composer's
Benighted gift. There is, too,

Always the possibility that he was better
Than his material—or maybe Joan did
Meet a comrade named Lionel on the
Battlefield, and…whatever. Tchaikovsky

Wrote a literature of the senses, and
This opera is as rich as you will ever know.
We are here, now and forever. The curtain
Is rising on the magnificent "Entr'acte."

Cole Porter's Son

When the pills don't work anymore,
And the one that you adore

Is slippery as an eel,
I can bet how you feel.

Don't have a seizure.
Make it a little easier,

When the liquor has turned you green—
You know what I mean.

When the food is making you sick,
and the love that makes you tick

Is getting to your ticker,
Don't lay it on any thicker.

Think only of this:
You're just as hot as piss,

Whatever you happen to be.
When you can't manage to see

What's the use any longer,
I swear you're getting stronger.

When the one you can't do without
Is always gadding about

Like a beautiful wolf,
And you think that you have proof,

Think about who you are.
Back when you were a star,

Could you know you'd be a comet?
I know someone who'd want it.

Early '80s

Alive in the Hamptons

"It's so beautiful in here," mutters Doug Crase,
Wandering off into the bedrooms. "I can't bear it."
You're pretty nice, too, Doug, as is Bob Dash

At the sink, handsomely snapping string beans
For our light salad lunch, to be followed by
Sun all around this afternoon. What a picture!

I can't bear it, either, this country-bred plangency.
It's so different from what lies in wait in New York:
The eyes-off overcrowding, fetal-position solitudes,

Hot Hispanics, spiritual hives, geysering fire hydrants—
Phew. "Hi, plants," says Doug, wandering back in.
"We *do* live on a nice planet." Does that include Manhattan?

Never mind. "I'd like to speak to Betsy about those
Japanese cherry trees and why she planted them."
Not knowing exactly what Doug is talking about, to Bob,

I still find it wonderful, still sigh to live this way.
Doug goes on about the Japanese a little. Bob clears his throat
Twice over the cool salad. "This is going to be good." Me too.

He's Dead

Bruce, my landlord, tells me
That Mr. Shapiro died Saturday.
According to Bruce, Mr. Shapiro
Was sitting on a bench near Riverside
Park, chatting with a friend, and,

In the event, simply checked out,
Without a sigh. "Good way for the old man
To go," says Bruce. I agree. I didn't
Want to ask what's going to become

Of his apartment, even though John
Needs one. Let me pay my respects
To Mr. Shapiro as best I can. I
Won't see him coming and going
On the stairs anymore, or exchange

Gruff hellos. Mr. Shapiro died,
And the autumn afternoon was
A little bit colder, a little bit
Crisper. John couldn't afford it,

Anyway. Leaves skittered to the
Sidewalk as Mr. Shapiro died.

Rich McK.

I met him in a bar
A few years back, around
Christmastime. Of course, I had
Seen him in church—blond
Hair, a deviant cherub's face
With inset azure eyes—
And wondered from afar.
But now I was actually talking
To him, this Episcopal dream—
"Oh, that's where I saw you—church."
We left together. We did,

For the usual reasons, heart
To praying heart. Later
I played Judy's then rare 1957 album,
"Alone," for him, which he
Listened to thoughtfully,
Especially "Blue Prelude." I

Saw him at St. Ignatius' some
Months later. We engaged
In forced conversation but
Hardly spoke, his eyes went
So dead. He's in England
Now, studying for the priesthood.
Funny, though. The last time
I saw him, with others at
Coffee hour, he was suddenly friendly.

He said, "Oh, I found that Judy
Garland album and bought it. I play it
All the time." Blond hair. Azure
Eyes. I didn't think he could have guessed.

Favorite film director: Alfred Hitchcock
Favorite singers: Leontyne Price
                             Billy Idol

Favorite idol: Iggy Pop
Least favorite idol: Elvis Presley
Favorite Pop: My father,
                             For sure

Favorite poppers: The real ones,
                             Which you can't
                             Get anymore

Favorite hanger-on: Can't say here
Least favorite hanger-on: Bianca Jagger

Favorite comedienne: Carol Burnett,
                             When she's
                             Being funny

Favorite comedian: Cary Grant in
                             "North by Northwest"

Least favorite comedienne: Phyllis Diller,
                             Poor thing

Favorite food: Anything without peas
Favorite protein source: Huh?
Favorite actor: James Stewart
Favorite game: I hate Scrabble

Favorite riposte: "How long will this take?"
Favorite '60s memory: The Mamas and the Papas

Favorite character trait:	Total honesty
Favorite faded blond:	Eva Marie Saint
Favorite nuts:	Pistachio nuts
Favorite male blond:	Richard Thomas
Favorite work of art:	*Guernica*
Least favorite artist:	Picasso
Favorite book:	*The Double Dream of Spring*
Favorite movie:	"The Roman Spring of Mrs. Stone"
Favorite activity:	Going to bed
Second-favorite film director:	The crazed Brian De Palma
Favorite poet:	Emily Dickinson

The Confessions of Gerrit

I drink a lot of skimmed milk.
I use air fresheners in the bathroom.
I stare long and hard at handsome faces.
I'm afraid to ask for the real price of my work.
I write poems after midnight, well after.

I stay home alone on Saturday nights.
I have laid in a good supply of Tucks.
I've gotten fat to discourage AIDS.
I use a little pseudoephedrine to help me work.
I don't exercise anymore, except coming up the stairs.

I was bored by "A Clockwork Orange," the movie.
I pore over *The National Enquirer.*
I've read about 30 pages of Proust's novel(s).
I like Peggy Lee better than Ella Fitzgerald.
Doesn't that say something awful about me?

My parlor palm is dying, frond by yellowing frond.
I think I'm running out of things to confess.
I'm not St. Augustine or Gypsy Rose Lee.
I usually feel like an asshole.
I say, "Hi, guys!" to dogs tethered on the streets, and pigeons.

I write art criticism too fast to read it.
I don't always—but usually—enjoy Henry James.
Maybe Geraldine Page is my favorite movie star,
If I could just think of a few movies she starred in.
I hope I am very ambitious.

What Is Art?

What is art?
Late nights sans pot,
And people about whom
You care a lot?

What is art
But a living shade,
And a certain hopefulness
About making the grade?

What is art?
Paying it off?
Stifling the
Too-jealous cough?

What is art?
Can it be bought
With the guarantee
You won't get caught?

Who is art?
Is she a Mr.?
An anti-Communist,
A dope, a drifter?

Who is art?
Sir Walter Raleigh?
Or Pollyanna whom
For short we call Polly?

Who is art?
A man killed by bees?
A friendly but perverted
Desire to please?

What is art,
But a lost
Shakespeare troupe, Benvenuto
Cellini, Shelley Winters, The Group?

What is art?
Did it go unsaid
Until Friedrich Nietzsche
Declared God dead?

What is art?
Utter derision?
A new Job who
Will never get the vision?

What is art?
What about creation?
Do you really need
An explanation?

What is art?
Is it deep?
A dreamer in
A conscious sleep?

The Mirrored Clubs of Hell

All are ways of knowing oneself.
Sometimes they baffle, or, worse, rankle.
Sometimes I snore or miss out on a dream—
Success at last! That too, though, is grief—
Too many red stains in the dull snow of evening,
And, eventually, good reason to marry.

Driving down Chikopee Lane now with my Dad.
When with my Dad I still feel,
"What's the difference to what I do?"
Is love so lost to go on so long?

I'd enjoy a big pill or a smoke now,
But I'm clinically maniac-depressoid,
And the combination might be unwonted.
I need room to kick out and break in.
He's loud, insinuating, rubber-lipped—
He's kind of a Daffy Duck in that respect,
But I wouldn't serve him for Christmas dinner.
We are now entering an exclusive danger zone.

"Men's sport bottoms and the will to live,
Next floor!" Time to be a primate at last!
But for me, that's like naming a boy Lynne
Or a girl Conchita or a dog Divine—
Any step you take'll trip you up good.
"Men's breviaries and a mother's prayers, this floor!"
I will both sue and settle to show my new interest,
That life is as precious as the schemes we all forget.

Judy Garland and Frank

In the picture in *People*,
Judy sits with Frank,
Circa the late 1940s,
Neither of them
Looking quite comfortable,
Or high, or particularly
Hollywood. Although Judy's face,
Even as early as her late
Twenties, is beginning to display
A certain cruel chastening
Of the soul and heart,
Which "speed" will inexorably
Wreak. Frank Sinatra

Is holding some kind
Of document in his hands—
A contract?—bony fingers
Folded around it, held length-
Wise against his leg.
His head is turned to Judy
In concerned conversation.

Who wouldn't be concerned?
This home-grown little sparrow
Of song betrays cud-brown
Eyes of mystic sadness,
In modish black silk
With big flowers on it,
Arms flopped haplessly
In her lap, one hand

Over the other, both
Benumbed with rings.

She wanted to
Marry Frank, it seems.
At least, *People* says
As much. Frank wouldn't
Buy it. "Was she pretty?"
I sometimes ask myself.
Or is it just me?

It is just me, and
You, and you, and them,
The thousands or millions who
Flocked to her '40s movies,
Tore through news items
On her raging suicide
Attempts, watched her fail,
Tongue-tied, on '60s TV,
Caught her croaking, soaringly,
At the Palace in '67.
Soon, there was darkness.
Anyway, I refuse to frame
This paparazzi picturing
From Los Angeles studio vaults.
I have another one up. This is
Too intimate, too upsetting,
And happenstance to frame
Over the dining table
On my wall. Frank is now
A dull legend,
As portrayed. Judy is
Still a dream, as given.

For My Father at 67

I'm so much like you, at last,
And I'm glad. I love you—
No matter the stern judgments,
The grave lapses of attention,
As if you were living in another,
Even more farfetched world.
The five a.m. waking. A slight limp

From football glory days.
I grew up thinking I was like Mom,
And Janice like you. Not the case.
What clinicians might call depression—
The sometime deafness, the sharp laugh—
It's everything I ever wanted,
To be like you, as I am as I grow older.
Someday we'll both find ourselves

In Paradise, and you will hug me firmly,
And I you, and give Mom a kiss.
I promise, by then I'll make it up to you,
Being both a poet and an art critic.
We even showered together once,
When I was little. It comes to something.
I'm so glad about this
Bright, new marriage of two despondent sons.

The Violent Tax-Protest

1
Setting up shop
For the night. "Things
Have a way of turning
Out so badly." Waste
And disappointment,
Dissipation and shame. Waste
And humiliation and hot,

Ivory tears. I know
Pretty well when I've been had—
The charm, the chill, the congress—
Good, and up to no good. Until I
Fall back against the fallow
Pillow. Until I fall back like
Raggedy Andy alone, shooting scag.

2
"Don't depend on Switz-
Erland." Sister Donna tore
Through her book of days,
A scarlet oak leaf falling
Out at the selfsame spot
Where one night she had
Saluted a full moon.

Psychopathic *is* telekinetic.
"The urge to merge," wrote Cole
Porter, "with a splurge." I

Can't stand when that
Happens. I go, "Oh, no."
A lady in constant pilgrimage
Wipes back the fog of sweat

3
Feeling both mutant
And delirious. It's such
A small world, Herb,
At such an enormous cost.
I'll do it, though, if I have
To stay up every night
Between now and New Year's Eve.

Thank God for my thinking.
Thank God for my only
Love, my continuing work,
Which, alone in the klieg light,
Staring out over a sea
Of popular strangers, will pay
Me back, occasionally,
In pure concupiscence
And mercury, at her pleasure.

If one is born too lonely to feel—
If there is an exacting correlation
Between the way we act
And the way they deal—

If no one really minds
(And no one should,
If often they do)—
If I could sensibly love you—

If kindness is a farce
And joy a mutation—
If no one can say,
And having said that, turn away—

If you care for me now,
Despite luck and elation—
Not minding when or how,
As if the wind could smell snow—

If death has a face,
And that face is death—
And if you shouldn't pay any attention
To what the Lord hath saith—

If, where there is generosity,
There is still room to give—
If our twisted sympathies
Would just allow us to live—

As if Jerusalem were the kingdom
Of no turning back—
If what can be put in writing
Could be put into words—

If the sun is black
With a million birds—

If everything means something
Which cannot be known—
If you scan the horizon
For cloud or stone—

If the sky is swollen
From too much rain—
If most things happen
For more than gain—

What if the trees kneel,
Or if there is no new, dumb song?
What if I wait for you,
And wait too long?

If you love me,
Wear your heart on your sleeve—
But only if what you believe
Is truer than what you discover—

Only if there is time enough,
And if you'll stay and be my lover—

If you'll hang around
And rehearse with me
That heart's hieroglyph—
If.

Papaver Somniferum

The room is cooling off,
After late-afternoon hots,
And this on a sixty-degree day—
Sun-absorbing blacktop above. I am stricken
At the thought of tomorrow: I have to both
Drop off, and later pick up, the laundry,
And write at least one *Art in America*
Number—for which, however, I have already
Laid a feasible verbal groundwork. But so
Much is going on there after the coup d'état,
And they say they've lost my reviews.
What can the redoubtable Elizabeth Baker do?
Find my reviews. It is not a good thing
To have had them go astray. It is not
A good thing, no, not a good thing
To stay up every night until four a.m.,
And sleep, helled-out, until two in the afternoon.
The world, perhaps, is not a good thing—
Perhaps. I used to trust in it
Blindly; I knew no higher law
Than the "good things"—sex, booze,
Sleeping pills, being unrequitedly
In love—although ceaselessly having it returned—
For seven years. But this
Wasn't enough. I saw
The moon fall. I fed angels.
They locked me up
For three scarifying weeks in the balmy
Spring of 1978—I had my 28th birthday

Party at Brunswick Psychiatric on the Island,
The true Amityville Horror
(Actually, it was rather country club)—
And then again for two weeks
In the fall. Ah art. Right now I see
Wolfgang Amadeus composing, pushing
A billiard ball away from him
Across the pool table, getting a few
Notes down with his quill,
Then sending the ball away
Again as it returns. I eat grapes,
Even a little real sherbet, to
Stay on my diet. I'm worried about
The painkiller my dentist probably
Won't prescribe, even though
I am in pain. I say the former
As good luck. My mother used
To call me a worrier—"You *think* too much!"
Yes, it's much cooler in the apartment—
Although I don't think Percodan
Was exactly a solution Mom would champion—
But still my mother was right.
I look at life through an emotional glass-bottomed
Boat, afraid, and afraid not to be.

Intermission

Song

I love him in the depths of my heart.
I love him with the warmth of the sea.
He will be there when I start
And finish my history.

He is not here tonight,
Neither can he be.
He will be there when I start
And finish the mystery.

Things are changing for the best,
Sort of. The days pass on wheels,
Enigmas of enigmas.
I don't hear the voices
So often now, which is nice,
And not so nice,
In the sense that
They were true—if
Autocratic—friends.

Sometimes the things
Real people say to me
Are far more wounding.
It is not their fault.
They are starved
For the sun of the Indies.

Charles Darwin never really
Awakened from his dream—
The dream of you and me as eternal.
Darwin grew to weigh
Well over 300 pounds,
Which might have been the karmic debt
He had to pay for his assorted insights.

Turtles as close ancestors!
Long-legged, fat black spiders
Having any knowledge of the soul!
We will wait for another messiah.

He will arise from the ranks
Of the disadvantaged, the hunted, and foresworn.

Isn't life a firefly,
Translucent in its brevity,
But dumb as the halo
Round the head of a saint?

Sleep is an inheritance
I don't want to come into,
But will, if I stay up
Just a little longer.
"Come with us," whisper
My fingers. I think money
Has changed radically in nature and value
Over the years. I still love it.

Life is not good.
At least, life is not kind.
Yet things are getting better.
I don't see hallucinations anymore,
As a rule. My tears fall, run, course,
Do everything but settle.
Was that the scream of the witch
Of the night of the witch I just heard?

Spiders and ducks, just think!
Keep July under wraps,
Until August, when the worst
Is both over and just beginning,
Like the moment of love.
Doubts assail me

Like shambling beggars on the subway.
Glass shatters noiselessly.
My fears crown me king of the May.

I suffer beyond my means,
As always. The dog swivels his head
And bites at his flea collar,
Which is strange, because
I don't have a dog,
With or without fleas.

I was about to say
That it was turning out to be
A nice evening,
Until I looked out the window.
Have you ever noticed
How donating to your favorite charity
Never pays off?
You are my favorite charity.
If you go, the moon will fail,
And plunge, gasping,
Into the Baltic Sea.
It's an anniversary you're
Sure to remember—
Up the pearl staircases of summer,
And down again,
Never coming back,
The paramount good
Being good that loves even us.

Mysticism Sacred and Profane

When night comes in its terrible loneliness,
And you are at your various dinners and parties,
Remember me in my awful one-and-onlyness,
Sweethearts, jerks, jerkers-off, smarties.

Here I am in this dank little world of mine,
Sick, or stinking drunk, wanting to be with you.
Maybe you will read this and take it as a sign
Of what, in life, to do and not to do.

If so, remember that in my hard-won wisdom
I am by far the stupidest creature that ever lived,
As dumb as Ganymede when the moon has kissed him,
Dumb like a fox, and able to forgive.

So just forget about me. And in that passing,
Enjoy yourself as you never have before.
I am all here in my woeful wiseassing,
Scared as a boy, and, like him, wanting more.

Psycho

Nothing can represent the sadness I feel.
No explanation can explain the way I've ended up,
Alone and afraid, alone on this stool,
Alcoholic, crazy, homosexual, cruel.

"She sits alone with a toad at her feet.
The tint of the afternoon makes her sad.
She looks at you without a flicker of recognition.
She is not depressed. She is mad."

No one dares to call me anymore.
Gainsaying as it seems, I keep on living,
Having long ago lost the courage to take my own life.
I walk home, skipping, thinking vaguely of a wife.

"Melancholia gets up and paces her chambers.
Tonight she will drink until she is utterly inept."
No one knows me, whom they long ago lost the name for,
Bleeding from behind, hideous adept.

Jailbait

The Tears Dry, the River Freezes.
"Oh Mom I Love It When He Teases."

The Clouds Mend, the Plants Apply.
"Will I Be Old as a Tree When I Die?"

The Beast Moans, the Beast Frozen in the River.
Girls Do What Boys Can Only Shiver.

"Oh Mom, Mom—That's the Stuff!"
I'm Like Her Man to Her but Not as Rough.

Incautious

That magic was just careless,
An era in which stability
Had increasingly sired stagnation,
Wax dolls left out in the wet
To get wetter—an eye here, another there,
Dangling obscenely from a sparrow's beak.
He turned the pages of his boys' Baedeker
Upside down—the Baedeker, that is—in
What pacesetters would later come to call
"Preferred action." The meeting

Broke up with the squealing
Of chairs, a tiny, hesitant choke left near
The center of the toothpastelike
Implement, the time capsule. And we could,
Too. Shock tactics were what were
Needed now, which bewildered even the administrators,
On this typically bizarre, scorching Sudanese
Evening, generously scented with true mint.

John

John is painting, or was,
Blacking out the nuclear power
Symbol I said looked
Like a Keith Haring. Or was:
Now he's skittering around,
Cigarette dangling from his lips:
Now he's sitting down
Again, shaking the little bottle
Of gold gouache. More painting,
Or drawing in paint. The apartment

Is a microwave, simply put. I
Hate July. My feelings for upcoming
August are unprintable. "Pacific
Overtures" on the air: "It's called
A bowler hat." Now John is
Sitting up straight, brush in hand,
Looking at what he's considering,
His ash blond hair all over his
Head a brush fire, out.

The Light of the World

If somebody asked me
Who my main influences
Had been…but who
Would want to know
An inane thing like that?
I ran around to three galleries
Today. I couldn't find hot cross
Buns in any of four groceries.
Tonight I walked out on
Easter Vigil at St. Ignatius.
Broadway this weekend eve
Was alive! Not just with creatures
Of the night, like me, but lilies
Languishing in their stalls,
Loud children's cries, dogs leashed

Senselessly to parking meters,
Yuppies, winos, bums. I missed Mass,
And the Eucharist. But I got
The *Times* early. Why do
Such pomp and ceremony
Have to crowd out
So simple, so basic a memory?
It's too late now.
Time to write a nice
Important poem, and this,
Guys, is it. Easter gladness.

Les Temps Fugitifs

Time is kind, sometimes:
You're twenty minutes late, and so is she.
Time is always right, not too bright,
Never out of synch, as we tend to be.

The days of the waltz relied on time,
But its use in today's music remains unclear.
You move into a house, you find a spouse:
Cheap excitement. Like music, time is queer.

I have a sliver of glass in my foot.
It's taking time to needle it out.
The needle stings, but nothing brings
It up. That's what time is about.

"Gnat" is in the vocabulary of time,
And "now" for anxious nuns.
Or is it "always"? The clocks in the hallways
Don't stop, chime like guns.

The Neutering

The definite allure of
The wayward woman
And her kind belting out
"Not Since Nineveh"
In a musical-comedy Arabian Nights,
Entices like the death's-head
Of a cobra, yet is
Exemplary for our time.
We are all wayward, "today"
People, some in pursuit
Of notoriety, some milk and honey,
Others a drink, more, lovers,
A few with genuine talent,
And a few truly lonely
In their modish dissemblings.
I have nothing left:
No opera tickets or reason
To go to the opera, no
Friends who don't kid
Me, no electric fence
To rest my weary head.
I slept through my hair appointment
Today, liking it long and wavy
Unconsciously, I guess,
Fancying in a dream, perhaps,
That I was an upright King David,
Not a fallen Bathsheba, that
For once my sound beauty and judgment
Exceeded my sour intellect,

And the sun my night.
There is no need to pray now,
And no good reason not to.
So it goes, getting funnier and milder
Everywhere. There is a cheering
Multiplicity of true answers,
Chancier decisions, and thatched-cottage
Latticework to all this, but no detente,
The situation we must
Truly strive for, if we're to win.
Wayward men rule the world,
And, according to Jesus,
They are cardinal. When they see us
Coming, the dead will fly,
And the merciful be shown unnumbered
Mercies. Not since Nineveh, no.
Not since I loved you, and you had to
Move away, out of the shadow
Of a great emerald cross. Crisis breeds
Great men, not stronger ones,
And devout, not excruciated,
Women. He who does is a class subdivision
Of the type who birthed this thing,
Groaning mightily and forcefully
Through cavernous halls. Do you
Know what I mean now?
Truth answers truth,
In the dream, and is
Irreconcilable with late summer,
With August's sweaty providence,
With our prudent genius. Genius!
In a world of wayward men,

Here surely are the knights,
Incontrovertible and simple,
Even a little bit dumb,
Like the kind of puppy we love.
There—that's a square deal.
Not a word is wasted,
Not a pause extended, from time
To bottommost time. I watch all
Of you, my nose to the windowpane,
As you gather joyfully around
The Yule wreath, snow melting
Like tears on my eyelashes.
I drive on. I think of strange women,
Women volunteers, *The Thinker*, the musical theater,
Knowing He will choose
The time for me to die, to die
Appropriately, if not easily.
Ease has nothing to do with it,
Which is the problem with wayward men
And women. You get to half believe it.

Pfitzner's "Palestrina"

for John Ash

This is love—take it or leave it.
Or that's what a wet, mild December evening
Full of black orchids seems to be saying,

And adds, "The fire god ate my heart."
The holidays: somehow I feel there's no longer
A price on my head. This is bracing,

As were the almost certainly professional carolers
Outside my window last night, caroling.
John Wells strained to see out the windows;

I had to pull him back.
I am, I'm afraid, always pulling John back,
Or is that just part of the great blue litany

We chant to ourselves after the fact, the next morning,
As a sop to myriad guilts, then peacefully die?
By noon, we've restarted the campfire, though.

Anyway, I perceive this somewhat cryptic missive
As part elegy, part freewheeling homily,
Part tribute. The tribute is not to you, but your stars,

And your odd niceness and restrained honesty.
You are all late youth, still devoutly favored,
And your talent is as sensitive as the moon.

Like you and unlike you, I have my share of problems.
They seem worst at festive times, especially the fact
That the people who had consummate faith in me

For so long, I've suddenly lost all faith in.
Out the windows, I hear a girl vomiting—
Or at least, coughing and hacking, as in the movies—

And aren't movies generally slick cut-and-paste jobs?
We take our time, and time is not to be slighted.
I guess it's that way for everyone we know:

I guess we're all malcontents, dizzy stylists.
So were Titian and Terbrugghen, Vincente Minnelli,
Veronese and Vermeer, Laurel and Hardy.

Which is to say, John, I'm glad you're back,
To play the quasi-gentleman with, to snarl and snipe at,
Or share a downscale dinner, or a very liquid brunch.

We know who we are, whose hearts the fire god has eaten.
Still, it's best to have a little faith.
I see the Christmas star is rising above the condos.

Recently

Jimmy

Jimmy, with
The flame in
The eye, the
Shotgun laugh,
At times, the
Hunter's gaze

Wearing your small
Neat blue tennis
Shoes out to
Dine at Onini's on
A stormy
Thursday night.
Random House

Just sent me
Your new
Book, and I
Devour it, Jimmy, Jim,

James Schuyler,
One of the
Few people I know
I don't mind
Being a genius.

Labor Day '87

for Ellen Adler

Oi. Then again, God.
There have been worse days,
And much better—if only
We could take roll call
At the start of each blistering morning,
Make a list of people you'd like to but couldn't.

This poem is in VHS Hi-Fi Stereo,
Ellen, although it sounds something less,
Like maybe an old Emerson, non-optimum
Performance. Better get out and walk home,
Or hitch. I'll be a male Claudette Colbert.

Sex. I actually started having sex
Again after it dawned on me
How dangerously far into Ken Russell-land
I've been moving. I was just kidding—
About the sex, I mean.
Ken Russell is a permanent problem.

Something will come of all of this,
Ellen A., just you wait and see.
Your brush sadly, affluently invokes
Spirits of mum and pom-pom,
Fructifying order and love in one.
I'm glad to find you alive here in East Suffolk this evening.
Oh to be two highwaymen on a night like this!

Two Notions

John's lying on the futon
He's still got his boots on

We don't say a word,
So words go unheard

Somewhere in the night
Are torture and delight

Thank the Lord, a ways away
I think gibberingly about today

And its jarring, sweet events
Receding from my mind like Berbers with their tents

John looks rather handsome
In the dark. We could prance some,

Talk, smoke, swing,
Tied together by nothing less than the Sting

But John is now lying on his side
A man and his devoted pride

And I'm just about to go off
Into my world of dreams and show off

No two could be stranger,
So thoroughly out of danger

Join us, as we disembark
And are enshrined here in the dark

For My Father at 71

There is no good in grief
Not a hair, not a leaf

The terrible sense of urging
The horrible, ritual purging

And the fear of crushing debt
Your room at last is out to let

It's a terrible burden
And life has no final word in

The matter, at last.
Future is empty past

No commutation of sentence
Each second is gravely Lenten

The moon beating fitfully down
Surrenders her diamond crown

There is no good in watching
True fate once again botching

Another mortal matter,
But to watch your hopes shatter

There is no good in grief
Only rabid disbelief

And the spreading of ancient pain
Like a wet, dirty stain

And a horse and a cadaver
No life. No endeavor

The wind finally stayed
The casket once again mislaid

We have no voice in this
We have no choice in this

But to pun and rhyme.
There is evil in time,

And there is no good in grief.
Love is a careless thief.

To Liza Minnelli,

unrivalled queen of
disco grief—
ca. 1990, no less—
who is, at
this moment,
probably as benighted
and confused as
I am, and
my lamb.
I miss summer—
and I don't
mean Donna—
sometimes, when
it's just "Let's
go do
something *else*
bad to ourselves,
shall we?"
Things to do

tomorrow:
don't call *him*.
Your eyes look
sullen and fearful,
where once they
were only handsome,
then, when your eyes
were unenshrouded?

Getting back
to that: I miss
the seasonal madness,
August's poor-lad-ness!
September's hot
green afternoon,
its unequivocal nerve.

I heard the
birch sing,
then, and
the Choctaw, too,
and a tiny
chorus of pearl.

I sometimes think of
this life—this
bewilderingly mortal
life—as a continuing
parody of itself,
a series of
unintelligible
blips and bleeps
on the video screen of fate,
ending in complete
video blitz.

Liza, "if there
was love,"
would that
be enough?
Your new disco

tape is retro-
everything. And
"if" makes the
refrain read "were"—
but that's rock
for you. Liza, I'm
going through
the holidays like
beer through
a sailor. Some

invisible protective
layer, though, lies
between my terror
and my reason.
I'm feeling nauseous—
I'll never take
aspirin again, I swear.
You're never really
thinking of the
other person. I know,
from my own sobriety,

out of the
dark, again,
into scorching light.
Your tape
was, by the way,
sold out
at Doubleday
this afternoon.
Streisand's new one

just sat there,
in droves.

Who would
claim to
be that popular
and not?
I wish
I were
even pitiable.
I am?
And more?
Like animals, Liza,
we'll need
endless patience.

Omnivert

The window is slightly open,
And the venetians are partially up.
Maybe the sun will wake me tomorrow—
God knows, nothing else will.
It's hard to believe it's only eleven minutes
Since funny Joan Rivers went off the air.
The Fauré "Requiem" comes as culture shock.
Speaking of which, or on some
Variation thereof,
J. J. Mitchell died of AIDS
Last Wednesday, I found out
Over dinner with Jimmy Schuyler
And Darragh Park tonight.
Dramatically, my head fell to my chest,
A reflex memorial to
Tears that don't have a way to come.
Thus the Fauré, probably.
There's more: a nuclear plant meltdown
In the USSR today, outside of Kiev,
Killing untold scores of
People. Europe is worried sick,
And a radioactive cloud is expected
To drift down the west coast of the USA soon.
Joan made no mention of it tonight
In her monologue. I call her Joan
The way we talk about Johnny, but also
Because I knew her in younger days—
Hers and mine—as a motormouth interviewee
Who liked guys. She acquitted herself

Well of the "Tonight" show, though,
I think. Earlier, Jimmy was cantankerously
Witty, flint-eyed, and slightly put upon
By existence, like the Jimmy ideal.
And Darragh—high-toned, silvering
Temples, with just that touch of hectic
Hauteur that endears him to all.
But I don't understand about J.J.,
Or Aladar, who's taking it all
As if in the last reel of "Dark Victory,"
Which I don't mean cruelly—
It's a great movie the first time you see it
At 17, or for some of us, younger.

What's gone so radically wrong?
And who's the next to hit the fan?
If it's me, this has to be
A great one, which I doubt—
You can't always call the shots.
Jimmy's new book, *A Few Days*, someone commented,
Is at times so personal as to be unreadable.
That's right—like death, like the invalid's last wish
Worn as a Pierrot pin that night
On the lapel of a navy blue blazer
Under the huge domed light show at The Sinner.
"Isn't that a star?" Jimmy insisted, as we stood outside
On the sidewalk, looking up to the sky,
Waiting for Darragh inside to finish parleying
With John Ashbery and Pierre Martory,
Later arrivals, at another table.
"Why is there only one?"

Our Imaginary Friends

for Richard Roth

Stress is preeminently
For people in trouble.
To think he was 13
When he wrote his first *Adonis*!

Or was it a small "Diana"?
These things do not follow,
Being things, not useless thoughts,
Destined for rigor and return.

I just realized,
If anyone were to walk in here now
The first thing they'd see
Would be the album,
On top of the stack by the door,
"Barry Manilow:
Grandes Éxitos en Español."

Why did I have
To buy that?
And what are "éxitos"?
Showstoppers, I
Shudder to think.
Poetry is,
If nothing else,
A transcendental ego blowout,
Some new salve flown in on
Private chartereds, from Atlantis.
You debate this and that,
Proving a "nightmare scenario"

Of some kind to be both the best
And the worst possible.

But a nightmare scenario
Can be fun—if never,
Ever played out, on bone beach,
Or scum-soaked pond,
Or land.

Sometimes I like art so much
I feel like throwing up—
None of this Henry Geldzahler-
Migraine-in-front-of-the-
First-Gorky shit—the *works*.
Where's balm for the sting
Of a lifetime spent on wing?

It was, and is, a curious fit,
Although not a spurious fit, entirely.

Have you ever known
A good "good man"?
I took it
From the captain,
And gave it back
To the captain.
I don't drink anymore,
But no one cares.
The sun sets,

Softly, a dove nesting
Restlessly in
Her own coos.

From the Book of Daniel

Oh my lord, by reason of
the vision pains have come upon me,
and I retain no strength.

I am glad,
because I am
a river to
my people,
a service that
the wishful
cannot buy.
The sky troubles
me, like women.
Prosperity will
come, at my pleasure,
if not my leisure.

She didn't understand
Aramaic very well.
So she came clean.
Like certain very famous people,
movies are not only
the seminal 20th-century
art form—they are
the only one—
along with movie music.

They are like dreams.
I am convicted of this idea
more and more, as I travel
around the blue and
green land,
or roam, rather,

in my boots and sack,
across the great northern
continent—Iowa, Pennsylvania,
New Mexico, New Jersey—
always a brilliant bit
of soldiering, night
beleaguering its angels
with comets, stars askew
in a rare heaven
of blue henna rinse.
But it's been made
so easy—the guy on
his knees for good, sobbing—
all of it within my reach
at last, this dissonant
martial air,
the golden keys of Dresden,
the charming man
in the one-piece bathing
suit. I have never seen
a sunset I didn't like;
have never seen (or heard)
the loon; often stared
at the moon, a silver embossing
on gold and black midnight.

And this is the national
climate, in which dessert
has become dinner; the
sky, translucent sea;
the fog a transparent
haze, a fake Monet,

artificial blue light
lighting the gateway to
the Emerald City, and nowhere
beyond. It's alcohol, you
know—worse than pure
folly, less than pure
reason—but it's actually
really sex. Everything is,
known, or dormant, both
the having and the lack of it.

Thus, the "program" ideal—
of "rigorous honesty"
about oneself—becomes
a clever fetish. And honesty
never clamored for the truth,
or even its approximation.
For instance, if I am the
prince, who is the prince?
Must stop now, or soon,
because, although I worship
you, you elude me. Must stop
soonish, although my life
is incomplete without you,
as if my fires had been chilled,
not warmed, by
the greater fires of your love.

The Fag

At its height,
it's a mystery,
at its depths,
a baptistery.
I am poor,
but I am
not meek. I
am in love,
but not with
you. This voice

you heard coming from
nowhere belonged to a handsome
younger man—but
aren't they all?—
with no mean impediment,
no sign of difficulty,
no species of delay
exhibited upon
considering the
loving request. If
it were honest,
it were true, if not—
best no beggaring
that description. He

heard a sound—
didn't so much
hear as notice—

and looked around.
The gold quatrefoil
glinted green in the silent
half-sun; the bearded
emissary from a
nearby land shifted un-
easily in his chair. The dice
were tossed—no-
one could possibly lose.

By combining Step !
with Step +,
you could have
what you wanted—
divide and concur,
I always say. But this
is wartime logic,
not fit for the ears
of God, or man, for
that matter. Although God,
God knows, is war-
like and sublime.

It's the sublime
part I appreciate,
and don't quite understand,
despite me.
At its height, it's
enervating,
at its depths,
a mere capitulating.
Dat's what I wanna

doodo ya—whad-
d'ya tink o'
dat? Sex is money,

money is hard,
and both are love.
That is all you
know, and all you get
to know. The harried painter
throws down her
brush, tossing her
chestnut mane in mid-
air. Was it a matter
of personal vision—
or just not being
able to see anymore?
She had scratched her glasses,
if truth be known.

                    No,
Jesus, I don't understand—
draw me a picture.
I am that stubborn,
that indecisive, and
certainly, that lonely.
Draw it on my lips.

Spring

after François Millet

O do not cry over unsung songs,
The daily routine of unrighted wrongs

Or things that beg your sympathy
But bring out strong antipathy

The wracking breath, the pitiful aim
To never more than, maybe, entertain

O do not say that you love me with your will
When time looks back with looks that kill

Worse, never stifle the rueful yawn
About your entire, golden existence as His pawn

A sower of the good seed throughout the land
Abandoned, as if he still could not understand.

Consider first the lesson of frost:
Fear faced, surmounted, fear crossed

The halting progress you must speed along
With hymns of damnation loud and strong

It's a foolish god who, dancing to static,
Claims the rest of the story to not be this dramatic

Sing, instead, a quasi-practical verse
To acknowledge that the cure that is worse than the curse

At least leaves you wanting to feel better
O make the bed, O mail the letter

Stand firm, friend, nor accept less
Than what is yours by right, and guess

"The Watchers"

I am looking at a movie
In which the monster is
Never seen—so far.
Human remains, however,
Are flagrantly on view.
Three school chums,
On their bicycles, in the
Woods, are set upon by fur
And fang; the fat boy's
Glasses, dropping to
The ground, drip scarlet.
A lady cop dies
Electrocuted against
A giant fuse box,
Her body jerking
Lustily to the rhythm
Of shooting sparks.
A school janitor
Screams and heaves,
Impaled on a rail.
All of them lose
Their eyes—bloody
Sockets smile
Where iris and cornea
Should gleam.

What exactly is
This movie about?
Man's bestiality to man?

The secret sharer?
And why no monster?
We should at least
Have the satisfaction
Of seeing this grisly
Evil; at least get
A closer look at this thing
Which guts and assails,
Who tears and violently
Probes, to wholly denude
Human beings, mere human
Beings of flesh and bone.

The mother is
An actress I've
Seen before; I can't
Place her.
No, she isn't.
The mother has just told
Son Corey Haim
"We're in this together."

Unfortunately, so are
We all. Sure, I get
A bang—probably of
Nefarious origin—out of
Watching horror movies
On my video recorder.
I'm always on the
Lookout for one or two
At my local video shop,
A few blocks down Broadway.

But as sure as I'm sitting
Here, talking to you—for
I can no longer bear,
One way or the other,
To watch "The Watchers"—
As sure as I sit here,
Typing along to
The Wagnerian background
Music, tired, nonplussed,
Disgusted, alive—I
Am shocked by the turns
This flick is taking, as it
Veers its way mindlessly
To some probably horrendous
Climax. I am
Shocked and outraged

By the sheer ugliness
Of it all, with its standard
Technicolor hues and
Substandard characters
And plots; its visual
Effronteries; its
Moral penury;
Its meanness—a mother
Unwillingly deprived of
Her child. Will I turn it
Off? Probably, no.
I am lonely. And, in some

Subtle, subterranean way,
The movie gives me courage,

Just by its viciousness.
It is a presence—like it
Or not—in my warm apartment.
It gives me the courage
To sit down and turn
To my typewriter,
And write you, and me,
An alternative,
Write away the horror,
Write away the blood,
The inevitable, quick progression
Of another American night.

I sat at the bedside,
as I'd seen my sister do.
I told him things
I never dreamed I knew.
I held his tired, skeletal hand
for ten or eleven minutes,
during which time I looked
at him, at the colonial rug
on the floor, at him,
at my copy of "Roger Rabbit"
in the bedroom bookshelves,
deciding I would ask for it back.

I kept wanting to move away,
but kept wandering into his room
nonetheless. There was a faint
odor of medicine to him
the day I left, but nothing rank or
objectionable, except the way death
had found him and was leaving him,
a helpless wanderer on the shores
of a much-vaunted immortality.

I'm not sure I care about
that kind of immortality, or if
there is any, or how it would feel
to be going there for good,
leaving behind the family you've sired
and your few friends, your proud

stake of land on storied Cape Cod,
your wife of a thousand days,
your children and their many problems,
and the stimulus that provided, and the pain.
Sunday night as I was leaving the room,
I turned around, and he was vaguely waving to me,
a gray arm raised above his head.
I waved back. I ran out crying.

Maybe this poem will make me immortal,
not mere death—a circumstance
none can escape or plan
or hope for or abandon.
Back in New York, I won't water the plants—
the two pathos that are left to me
after the condo's limitless skyward construction
across the street, blocking the sun
until two o'clock in the afternoon,
and then, having the sun for only seven minutes.

I can't get down to writing until ten
or eleven o'clock at night.
I spend hours crying, precious afternoon hours
when I would normally be doing my best work,
and I say, agreeing with myself,
"This is bad, huh?"
But what can the dumbstruck do?

I have to go to Los Angeles
a week from today on business—
or what I call "business,"
profitless pastime that it is—

and, although I dread it—
the arriving and the mutual staring,
the asking for and the sullen receiving,
the doing and forgetting—
I can't wait to go.
I tell people I like flying,
which is partly true,
and partly an addiction to
getting off the ground for good, for the moment.
Life, I think, is relatively harmless
until death; at which point you realize
that all you ever strove to give up
was not only the essence,
but the substance of it all,
and each time you tried to give it up
you moved a little closer to death's convenient vacancy.

Vacancy, indeed, is what I feel, and tragedy.
I hazily remember Henry James' dying words—
something along the lines of "Live all you can,
or you'll regret it,"
or maybe it was just "Live all you can."
Nor do I see my father approaching some czar of the heavens,
his hat in his hands, tears streaming
down his lonely face—"Well, what did you
do with your life, James? Excuse me—Jim?"
Although I sense he won't need a lawyer
to explain this, as I surely will.
I regret it deeply, all of it.
I regret being born, to see this.
I regret what I didn't say,
and what I did,

and what I might have,
and what I couldn't.
Now he'll never know
he was my hero.
Still, he was no ordinary kind of man.
He asked for the sun,
but was given instead the sunlit path he trod.

I know I'm not just imagining it anymore.
You are on my mind, loosely
And specifically, for I feel
An infinite identification with you.
What makes you laugh also moves me,
And what makes you angry
Is, to me, an interior governorship.

Why then haven't we met?
With a thousand things to do and forgo,
And with the earth inert, riding on the shell
Of a slow-moving, giant tortoise;
With nothing to be involved with
And not much time in which to do it;
With you home, and me home,
But both of us in separate places,
The day has yet to come, but must,
If I have my Eagle Scout compass set right.
You will grow older, and I feebler;
You will die and I will overexert myself,
Or I will die and you will know Pyrrhic victory,
But this much is as plain as night:

That I'm still waiting for you,
And you have a ways to go yet
On your sentimental itinerary.
It will come at no special time,
But both of us should approach it
As softly as a doe, with an open-minded inkling

Of the right course with which
To eagerly seek each other's approval.
That's the day I'm waiting for,
Am willing to live and fight for,
As much as life permits. I love you

In your absence, maybe even your absence.
Without yet knowing who I am,
Can you honestly say I'm wrong?
I court confusion in our anonymity.
I eat and breathe and happily pine,
And the summer cottage stands ready now,
Divested of all glamors but one.
If I had a number, I'd call you.
You'd know before you answered the bell
That this was it, in God's time and ours.
I'm so willing to be willing,
So ready to believe in anything but disbelief.
Come see for yourself the magic of our art.

Program

1
Night falls like
separate beads
of rain. There's
no refuge in
the wildlife preserve,
not even for wildlife,
although they try.

What do I want?
What do you want?
Are they similar?
Our enemies consumed
by waves of fire,
for instance?

Or is there some
better way to
determinedly proceed,
to not kick your neighbor
back, but to
possess him fully
in your love and art?

What have I
done lately
for the dead?
What ho, Fortunius?

Felonious? Fibber
McGee? It is
the loss of pleasure
that ails you so.

2
It is sadly
undeserved, though.
Hard work is
not hard. It is
ale for the soul,
although much depends
on the nature of the work.
Playing the reed—as just
one example—seems too much
like an ancient consolation
for a too-new grief.
So now is the time
to stop loving yourself.
We seem to think
in these beleaguered contemporary
days that it is hard
to love oneself—
but it is all too easy!

3
No one will talk to
me since I emerged from the
broiling seas, dragging
my great tail behind me
on the moonlit sand.

4

"Climb every Montaigne,"
he thought with a chuckle.
Play the Tchaikovsky
first, to be faithful
to your origins, faithful
to your beloved bias. That's
all very sage and wise,
but I think everyone suspects
anyway. You know I'm

5

The old ways do not
work any longer. Unfortunately,
neither do the new ways.
If I was indecisive before,
I had only to see his face,
the head whipped and
carved by the disease,
a vanitas skull with brown eyes,
superimposed on that other
face, of a young male lover—
not *his*, but him.
We are all still in
love with him, because, although
he could be cruel—well,
I guess that's some of it.

6

I am anchored on the brig
three of the boys were twice as big,
and why was he dancing that little jig?

Excuse me, I'm a bum—
do you have a cig?

7
I have no memory
of violence, only
shame. O such a
heavenly vine!
Our eyes glowed
sapphire pink.

The boys were allowed
to mingle with other
boys, but very few girls.
This was odd, because the
mean age of the
boys was 38.

How I'd love some
activity. Rowing.
Mowing. Hoeing.
Doing laundry, dirty
and clean. An imageless poetry—
why is that so hard?
I am not an image,
nor are you,
of anything we know.
We laugh; we turn
to music for the rest,
and are deeply gratified.
The atmosphere is right.

8

Oh! what a ghastly
vine! Anything the
eye may fall on—
"'Welcome home,'
says the chair"—
is fair game,
and that means Phrygia,
Claudette, Pseuodonymous,
Rosemary, Rosemary's baby,
Eponympous, and Epictetis
as well. You may

now go and swing
from a nearby tree.
No more harm will
be done you, for
tonight. But mind
the morrow, mind you.
Mind the writing, the not-
minding, the skillful
bending to the purpose,
as Nemesis whispers
liabilities in your ear.

9

I can't go on,
Jake—I'm losing blood
like the Titanic lost
life rafts—but you
can save yourself, even
at a hobble. Don't go

back there with me.
You have the chance to make
a fresh start. It takes
real courage to live in this
world, and you, of all people,
have it. That is attested to
by your very acts of desperation,
rendered illegible on the dull foolscap
of lack of inspiration,
in a crabbed scrawl, by
a precocious hand.
His mastery was growing,
although he would have
liked the chance to rephrase
that last, which seemed
to reveal a distinct *lack*
of mastery of the English style.
No more harm will be
done you as long as you
live. That is the pact
negotiated by the sun. That is the
pact affirmed by the way
the cards were placed,
all trumps and cross-purposes—
right card covers you,
cover card fools you silly.
"He is a gentleman, a farmer,
perhaps, who enjoys quiet
power"—which is as good
as it gets. Quiet power.

10
March, May—is it
the singer, or the sung?
Waldo sat in mummified
rapture, at the
sight of his

11
Ask Jan the date.
Include everything,
even sentiment, and, yes,
sentimentality. For
'tis a fine discourse
ye harp on the subject
of lost love, or love
forsaken or faked—
an imageless poetry,
that betrays neither meter
nor rhyme, nor even
gibbous free association,
but is the poem itself,
its nocturnal wakings
and wanderings, and comings-home
early to sleep.

Yet she is only interpretative,
not creative, genius.
That's where the chancre
Guh-naws, the unyielding
growth that has attached itself
to my clan in its later, landless
settlings. With the change

in the family fortune, I
had to quit my job.
My supervisor called me dunderheaded.
I said,

12
"I am but a conduit.
I am a medium for
these un*seen* forces
to operate through and by."
"Un*heard*, soon, also,
if I have my way."

"You dare not touch me.
My sisters died in the
bonfires of France,
burned as heretics
by men who knew heresy
to the marrow. I only
hear voices."

It's all my imagination.
You are all in my imagination.
Yet you are alive, and I.

I was so tired and mad,
by that time, he said
"Where should we have our
New Year's Eve party?"
and I shot back, "You
can have your New Year's
Eve party up your ass,

for all I care."
At this, he took umbrage.
I said, "Why not? You've
had everything else
up there!"

13
I grew then, like the
hawthorn, having been
early skilled in the wise
lispings of past ages,
the fleshly emendations
of soul through earth and birch,
our purest, grossest delicacies.
How many times can you
be told that you're bad
and continue thinking you're
anything else but? There's a
path to be followed here,
as undeservedly hallowed
as Beethoven's symphonies.
But have you heard the middle
quartets? Take another path,
similar to this easier one,
but anathema to the strong.
Who among you can deny the charity
I felt and acted on, in a vain attempt
to circumnavigate the tender promise
of your eyes? It has to do
with our whole generation—
we're all drug addicts. But
only some have visions, and only

few speak of them. I no longer
entertain mine, but I empathize
with those who do. It is undeserved.
An imageless poetry, beyond
shock or value—this would
be a true reward, to stand the
world on its hand. Strange—
reality started to seem omenic,
straight from the bottom of the
hidden well in the light-dappled,
jute-brown forest, in deference
to its mighty depths and squalors.

It is the loss
of pleasure that
ails you so. It comes
with the years, and their
increasingly weepy self-denials—
maybe you *should* love yourself,
after all. Because, if you
don't, who will? Who will
draw up for you in folds
and jewels the kaleidoscope
of your present situation?

Can you bear to give
the baby to an agency, or,
to *receive* one from the
agency, either? Life is pure
wit, or you lose yourself.
You start to worship sorrow,
and that—or so an old sot

told me—is a lot of "bullshit," I
recall was the word he used.
Because maybe you could help
someone else less fortunate—
a tiring bill to fill,
but timely. That's when death
seems to be leading nowhere,
when you help another heart—
heaven's gate, by now, being
overgrown with wild dahlias
and larkspur, gently intertwining
with the barbed wire and tacks.